Mladen Dolar
What's in a Name?

I0390993

Mladen Dolar
What's in a Name?

Published by:
Aksioma – Institute for Contemporary Art, Ljubljana

as part of the action *FREE Janez Janša*

Produced by:
Aksioma, **steirischer herbst**, Graz and **Artribune**, Rome

in the framework of **Masters & Servers**

Edited by **Janez Janša**
Proofreading: **Eric Dean Scott**
Graphic design: **Luka Umek**
Producer: **Marcela Okretič**

Ljubljana, November 2014

Contact: www.aksioma.org/contacts

Printed and distributed by: **Lulu.com**
www.lulu.com

ISBN: 978-1-312-65543-0

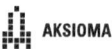   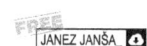 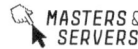

"What's in a name? That which we call a rose

By any other name would smell as sweet;

So Janša would, were he not Janša call'd,

Retain that dear perfection which he owes

Without that title."

Romeo and Juliet, II, 2, 43–49

It all began with Plato. The question of naming, of name calling, of the aptitude or ineptitude of names, their appropriate or inadequate nature, their capacity to hit the mark, their reference, their multitude, their force to evoke the thing, the impossibility to be disentangled from the thing, it all began with Plato, that is, with a singular name condensing the origin of so many of our concepts and our ways of thinking. There is already a certain paradox in this, involving this illustrious name, for philosophy in its endeavor towards conceptuality and universality, its striving for ideas, notions, theories, pure thought, ultimately hinges on a dozen, or two dozen, proper names forming the knots, pinning the universal to the most singular. Plato prominently features as the founding name to which a long string of concepts can be attached, providing them an anchorage in a name.

Plato's dialogue *Cratylus*, with the subtitle 'On the correctness of names', represents the first time in history that the question is seriously raised: What's in a name? A couple of millennia before Juliet, Socrates meets Cratylus and Hermogenes on a street in Athens, and Socrates is called upon to unravel this mystery, to intervene into the already ongoing discussion. Hermogenes was maintaining that names are based on a convention, an agreement of a community of speakers, and whatever the arbitrary agreement may be, it is the sole foundation of proper naming.[1] Cratylus, on the other hand, maintained that names must ultimately be based in nature, so that there would have to be a tie, an umbilical cord that attaches the names to the things named. Can it be that names are just arbitrary? Are some names better than others to designate the thing named? Can the names be true or false, and how is one to discriminate the one from the other? How do they refer to things? The specter of Juliet on the balcony is already there: Would the rose by any other name smell as sweet? Does the name affect its smell, or is it completely indifferent to it, or does its sweet smell affect the name and is it propelled by it? How do names smell?

Socrates, who is called in as a referee, first firmly establishes that there is a divide between true and false speech, and that names, being parts of

---

[1] "No name belongs to a particular thing by nature, but only because of the rules and usage of those who establish the usage and call it by that name." (384d) I am using Plato's *Complete Works*, ed. John M. Cooper, Indianapolis/Cambridge: Hackett Publishing Company, 1997.

speech, must also partake in this divide, that they cannot be simply indifferent, that there are ultimately true and false names. Furthermore, there must be an essence to things which the names must spell out[2] – things have their independent essence and names must in some way be dependent on this independent essence, although this essence, being completely independent, cannot be quite affected by the ways in which we happen to call things, but it is nevertheless not unrelated. Names are like tools that we need to get to this essence, and there can be tools which are more or less appropriate, and hence have a varying degree of truth or falsity. But these tools are not quite freely ours to choose, or to select better ones from, for the names are always given by some Other, the rule-setter, the lawgiver, the name-maker (389a), whose status escapes us. The names precede us, they are transmitted from generation to generation, and if one is to surmise about their origin and the beginning of the chain, then one would have to imagine some divine source, beyond the capacity of humans simply agreeing upon conventions – names are never

---

2   "Things have some fixed being or essence of their own. They are not in relation to us and are not made to fluctuate by how they appear to us. They are by themselves, in relation to their own being or essence, which is theirs by nature." (386d–e)

quite just a matter of consensus. The Other is there in the name, the instance of nomination beyond our reach, an instance which must have always already made the foundational gesture of naming back in time immemorial. When, in the biblical myth, Adam, the first man, named the animals, this didn't pertain to divine jurisdiction, but to human invention. Yet, the foundational Word was already there, outside of human range.

The supposed divine legislator is inscrutable, so one is always in a position to scrutinize the inscrutable, trying to disentangle his motives and assess the value of the names. "It's the work of a rule-setter, it seems, to make a name. And if names are to be given well, a dialectician must supervise him." (390d) So we need dialectics to gauge and evaluate the names, they have to be examined to see their possible foundation and their aptitude to spell out the essence of things.

If names had been given by some divine instance, by gods, where does the name for gods come from? Why are gods called gods, '*theoi*'? "It seems to me that the first inhabitants of Greece believed only in those gods in which many foreigners still believe today – the sun, moon, earth, stars, and sky. And, seeing that these were always moving or running, they gave them the name '*theoi*', because it was their nature to run (*thein*)." (397b) So we are a bit bemused to learn that 'gods' come from 'running', on the rather flimsy evidence that the two words happen to sound alike. And why are men called men, '*anthrōpoi*'? "The name 'human' signifies that the other animals do not investigate or reason about anything they see, nor do they observe anything closely. But a human being, no sooner sees something – that is to say, '*opōpe*' – than he observes it closely and reasons about it. Hence human beings alone among the animals are correctly named '*anthrōpos*' – one who observes closely what he has seen (*anathrōn ha opōpe*)." (399c) What about the soul, '*psuchē*'? It is what gives breath and revitalizes (*anapsuchon*) the body. What about the body? "Some people say that the body (*sōma*) is the tomb (*sēma*) of the soul, on the grounds that it is entombed in its present life, while others say that it is correctly called 'a sign' (*sēma*) because the soul signifies whatever it wants to signify by means of the body." (400c) So the body is at the crossroads between the tomb and the sign. What about love? "'*Erōs*' (erotic love) is so called because it flows in from outside, that is to say, the flow doesn't belong to the person who has it, but is introduced into him through his eyes. Because of this it was called '*esros*' (influx) in ancient times …" (420a–b) What about truth? "'*Alētheia*' (truth) is like some other names being compressed, for the divine motion of being is called 'alētheia' because it is a compressed form of the phrase 'a wandering that is divine (*alē theia*)'." (421b) So truth is like a divine drift, a divine straying – gods running a bit amok? And so on, and so on, for all the 130 or so etymologies, one fancier than the other, all proving that names are founded in some way, that they depict the thing they name, that they are in some manner like the thing they refer to, showing a certain fidelity to some of its key features, that they are always evocative, that there is no such thing as a neutral name.[3]

But the suggestions that Socrates proposes (and can he really mean all this?) are based on etymologies, the names are like compounds whose elements are already meaningful in themselves,

_____

3   Sometimes it's a bit tough and one needs a lot of exertion and cunning to find the connection, e.g. for *technē*, art or craft: "If you remove the '*t*' and insert an '*o*' between the '*ch*' and the '*n*' and the '*ē*' [thus obtaining *echonoē*], doesn't it signify the possession of understanding (*hexis nou*)?" (414b) Hmm – does it? If you remove some letters and insert some others, couldn't one prove just about anything? Where does this chain of associations stop, what is it based on, what does it prove? Is Plato pulling our leg?

the semantic value of a name is supported by the semantic value of another name, so that ultimately we are moving in a circle. If gods, *theoi*, comes from *thein*, running, where does *thein* come from? The origin seems to be on the run, running through the tight web of words, each one evoking others, sounding alike, but not just sounding alike, since the sound echo that reverberates among words coincides with the semantic echo, the similar sounds evoke similar meanings, they point in the direction of meaning which cannot be disentangled from the sound. Sounds are never quite arbitrary in relation to meaning, meaning is not indifferent to the sounds that happen to carry it – it runs with them.

But eventually one would have to consider the elements which are in themselves not semantic, like singular sounds, letters, phonemes, syllables, the components which form the building blocks of words and all semantic units. Would we thus arrive at something that is purely arbitrary? No way.

"Don't you think that just as each thing has a color or some of those other qualities we mentioned, it also has a being or essence? Indeed, don't color and sound each have a being or essence, just like every other thing that we say 'is'? ... So if someone were able to imitate in letters and syllables this being or essence that each thing has, wouldn't he express what each thing itself is?" (423e)

So letters, sounds and syllables could be like color and sound, evoking the thing, but expressing it better, not merely by its qualities, but by spelling out its essence. Colors and sounds have their craftsmen, the painter and the musician, and the craftsman that we are investigating is "the namer ... the one we have been looking for from the beginning." (424a) Can we name the namer? The name has to have a mimetic quality, it has to be like the thing, but also it has to pertain to logos, to the capacity of naming in such a way so as to spell out and express the essence. Letters (and phonemes) are the elements required for such a depiction – but why those? For instance 'r' (*rho*):

> "The letter 'r' seemed to the name-giver to be a beautiful tool for copying motion, at any rate he often uses it for this purpose. He first uses this letter to imitate motion in the names '*rhein*' ('flowing') and '*rhoē*' ('flow') themselves. Then in '*tromos*' ('trembling') and '*trechein*' ('running'), and in such verbs as '*krouein*' ('striking'), '*thrauein*' ('crushing'), '*ereikein*' ('rending'), '*thruptein*' ('breaking'), '*kermatizein*' ('crumbling'), '*rhumbein*' ('whirling'), it is mostly 'r' he uses to imitate these motions." (426d–e)

So there is no lack of evidence, words start flocking and mushrooming the moment one considers the evocative nature of, say, 'r'.[4] Words are like pictures of things, and if this analogy is to be carried further, then a picture depicts things by using colors that are similar to the colors of those things, and in the same way the elements of speech must bear similarity to what they depict. "Then by the same token can names ever be like

---

4   Derrida will make a big case, in Glas (Paris: Galilée, 1974), of the compound 'gl' and its particular nature of 'glue' (featuring also in Glas of the title), taking cue also from Cratylus, where Socrates expounds at some length on the nature of 'l' and its smoothness and softness, combined with 'g' (as in 'glischron', 'gluey'), "in which the gliding of the tongue is stopped by the power of the 'g'." (427b) Consider the case of Google, to extend Socrates' method to modern times, and its nature of glue.

anything unless the things they're composed out of have some kind of likeness to the things they imitate? And aren't they composed of letters or elements?" (434b) Names are like imitations of things, their images, notwithstanding their lack of imagery, and if there can be better and less good pictures, by the criterion of likeness and the capacity to conjure the thing they imitate, so can there be more or less appropriate names. Yet, there can be no perfect picture, since the perfect picture would be the double of the original, one couldn't tell them apart.

> "An image cannot remain an image if it presents all the details of what if represents. ... Would there be two things – Cratylus and an image of Cratylus – in the following circumstances? Suppose some god didn't just represent your color and shape the way painters do, but made all the inner parts like yours, with the same warmth and softness, and put motion, soul, and wisdom like yours into them – in a word, suppose he made a duplicate of everything you have and put it beside you. Would there then be two Cratyluses or Cratylus and an image of Cratylus?" (432b–c)

The specter of two Cratyluses appears, a picture so perfect that one cannot tell it apart from the original, the perfect double. The world inhabited by doubles would be uninhabitable, the world invaded by duplicates that one couldn't discern in relation to the original, the world of an art so perfect that it would redouble this world with its own images. But only god could supposedly be such an artist – or is it that even the weak human art, with all its flaws, nevertheless has the power of blurring the lines, infringing upon the real world of which it is but an image? Is this why Plato was so apprehensive and worried about art, to the point that he wanted to expel artists from the city? Once one engages on the path of replicas, even faulty ones, there is no stopping, for even the bad ones still possess the magic power of striking back at the original.

> "At any rate, Cratylus, names would have an absurd effect on the things they name, if they resembled them in every respect, since all of them would then be duplicated, and no one would be able to say which was the thing and which was the name." (432d)

Here we are. If there is a spot in classical philosophy where the project of the three Janšas is inscribed and anticipated, then it is this one. There is this passage in Plato which has been lying low for 2,500 years, secretly waiting for this project to emerge. We have it all there: names are imperfect images, for if they were to be perfect, then they would effectively redouble things, we would be faced with a double world where the mere name would be a perfect replica, and several entities bearing the same name would strike back at the original bearer of the name to the point that one couldn't be sure which is which. The project comes with a twist, though: if one cannot turn the name into the perfect replica of the thing, one can make the perfect replica of the name itself, the name can be cloned, so even if the name is an imperfect image, its tenuous and tenacious connection with the bearer is such that it clones the bearer. The one and only Janez Janša is, by the mere cunning of the name, multiplied by three more Janšas with the threat of becoming indistinguishable.[5] Cloning

---

5   If I were to try my own hand at the name Janša with the Socratic method of fancy etymologies, then, in the vein of Antiquity, the most prominent candidate for this would no doubt be Janus, the double-faced Roman deity of beginnings and transitions, the god of doors and passages, displaying a different face on either side. Is there a similarity by which the name Janša resembles its bearer? Here we have it, the double-faced entity, displaying >>>

the name blurs the lines, there is more in the name than a mere conventional marker.

Of course names are not perfect images and to imagine the universal reduplication would be an absurdity and a nightmare, but even in their imperfect rendering they nevertheless produce effects on the entities they name, hence Plato's struggle for the correctness of names and their proper foundation. In order to be a suitable name it has to involve a structural similarity to what it names, yet this similarity also involves a danger and threatens with confusion. Since Plato himself amply uses the analogy between naming and painting, one can refer to the way that he insisted on the perils of painting in Book Ten of the *Republic*: painting is merely the production of copies, actually of copies of copies, since the things of which one makes copies are already copies of ideas, but this is nevertheless dangerous. There is a mystery pertaining to all this: copies of copies – why the fuss? Why would such a slight thing as a copy of a copy cause so much concern

on the one hand the face of an orthodox communist functionary and on the other the dissident put in prison for subversive activities by the old regime; then the face of the prime minister and the leader of the right wing, and the face of the corrupt politician brought to court by the new regime; the national hero and the demagogic trouble monger. And above all, an entity of transition. Is this then an appropriate well-founded name in the Socratic vein?

and passion, even rage? Why would a doubling create peril? If copies and imitations have no proper reality, or a reality so much slimmer and dimmer than the real thing, why worry?[6] Why lose all this time and temper over something so minor, negligible and even contemptible? The trouble is that the copy, the imitation, has the strange power to affect the thing itself. Imitation strikes back, it impinges on the original, it has an impact on it. One makes a copy, not even that, a copy of a copy, and the world of ideas seems to be shattered, it has to be firmly defended against any such intrusion. Imitators can do more harm than they can possibly imagine, they can cause havoc by merely replicating, they can disturb the order of eternal ideas by making replicas of their replicas. Just as the sophists, those specialists in imitation, can undermine the true philosophy by merely mimicking it. Ultimately, Plato's fear was not that the copy, the imitation, the mimetic double, was but a pale and unworthy shadow of

---

6   Lacan considers this for a moment in *Seminar XI*: "[The story of Zeuxis and Parrasios] shows us why Plato raises against the illusion of painting. The problem is not that painting is an illusory equivalent of the object, although Plato seems to be saying this. ... Painting doesn't compete with the appearance, it competes with what Plato shows us beyond the appearance as the Idea. Precisely because painting is the appearance which tells that it is what creates appearances, Plato raises against painting as an activity competing with his own." (*Les quatre concepts fondamentaux de la psychanalyse*, Paris: Seuil, 1973, p. 103)

the real thing, his fear was that it was too close to the real thing, not separated enough from it, tied to it by an invisible thread that cannot be cut, the umbilical cord tying it to its supposed model, hence the model itself couldn't be cut loose from it. The danger is that they are so much alike that a supposed 'naïve observer' could easily mistake the one for the other.

By analogy, the same goes for names. The name may well be an imperfect image, but it is nevertheless too much of an image, the peril of the reverse effect is always there, it can undermine the reference, stain the entity it refers to. And what the Janšas have done is quite Platonic: if the name is to be considered as a pale copy of the thing named, they have done the copy of the copy, actually three copies of the copy. And if in painting the copy of the copy is always deficient in its rendering, then they have managed the remarkable feat of making the perfect copies of the copy, for the name can actually be fully replicated in all its facets, to the point of being indistinguishable. Should Cratylus have a perfect name, there would be two Cratyluses, what better name could one come up with than the precise double of the thing; but redoubling and multiplying the name conversely evokes the specter of four Janez Janšas.[7]

The artists' project was Platonic in its assumptions, and so was the reaction. Janša's party, SDS (Slovene Democratic Party) was highly disconcerted by this move, it showed a lot of annoyance and issued a number of dismissive and rather enraged remarks. Why would they fear the copies of the copy? No doubt they shared Plato's concerns, assuming that the name in some way affects the original, that it spells out its key features, so that there can be no neutral naming, and the multiplied names carried in themselves the features spelling out the essence, namely the Janšeity, which was hijacked by the mere multiple use of the name. Each Janez Janša was, by the name, endowed with the unfathomable essence of Janšeity, even more, this essence cannot be quite spelled out by any positive traits, it is only attached to the name, there is no other way of getting to it, so the use of the name dispossessed its original bearer of his singularity, his uniqueness, his ineffable being. The unease and

---

7   When the name change occurred in 2007, the three artists changed their Wikipedia entries, and the first thing that our oracle Wikipedia came up with was disambiguation. *Cf.* http://en.wikipedia.org/wiki/Janez_Janša_(disambiguation).

the rage witness that Platonism is alive and well in today's Slovenia, and SDS should be praised for subscribing to the ideas of Antiquity.

Let me say a few more things on *Cratylus*. Socrates is well aware of the traps involved in names, so his concern is ultimately not the proper foundations of naming in etymological twists and somersaults, but rather in getting to the proper foundations by bypassing names altogether.

> "But since there is a civil war among names, with some claiming that they are like the truth and other claiming that *they* are, how then are we to judge between them, and what are we to start from? We can't start from other different names because there are none. No, it's clear we'll have to look for something other than names, something that will make plain to us without using names which of these two kinds of names are the true ones – that is to say, the ones that express the truth about the things that are. ... But if that's right, Cratylus, then it seems it must be possible to learn about the things that are, independently of names." (438d–e)

So this is Socrates' dream, his ultimate aim: a direct access to things without the roundabout of names, a knowledge that could read things properly and adequately without this always deficient instrument of naming, involving distortion and bias, the infinite slide of sounds and meanings. Only on the basis of this clear capture of the essence independently of naming could we then judge what names are appropriate or not, lay down weapons and sign truce in this civil war of names. The proper knowledge would be the direct access to the nameless thing, without any use of names which are but intruders, the short-circuit between our mind and the essence which would get straight to the logos of things themselves without the logos of words – but doesn't logos essentially mean 'the word'? Can one get to the nameless word beyond all words without any words? And how could one testify to it without the words with which we are stuck? Socrates seems to shake hands with Juliet, who strives for love as the direct access to her beloved without the by-pass of the name. "'Tis but thy name that is my enemy," says Juliet, believing that one should get out of the regime of names to get to the pure love. But can one ever?

At the background of this silent and impossible enterprise as the ultimate goal, there is the glittering beauty of this dialogue, the beauty of endless punning, the endless wordplay, the endless poetry of words echoing other words, of reverberations of sounds and the concomitant reverberations of meanings.[8] From *Cratylus* to *Finnegans Wake*, there is but a step. This all may be fanciful and far-fetched, and there have been many ruminations about the status of this long exercise – could Socrates, and Plato with him, possibly be serious? Yet, at the bottom of it there is the insight that this entanglement of sounds and meanings presents the real of the name, the way that names refer to things quite apart from, and on the top of, the usual univocal designation. Synonymy, with multiple different words meaning the same, presupposes the univocity and unicity of meaning that can be expressed by various means. Homonymy, with the different words sounding contingently alike, presupposes the dispersal of meaning, its dissemination. The paradox of Cratylus is that it tries to pin down

---

8   "Hesitation between sound and meaning", this is how Roman Jakobson defined poetry, following Paul Valéry. What better testimony to this definition than *Cratylus*, despite and because of its epistemic endeavor which tries to disentangle the two, to get to the purity and univocity of meaning by means of the impurity and plurivocity of sounds.

the univocal and unitary meaning by means of homonymy, by the erratic nature of language which unpredictably lends itself to chance encounters. Episteme meets poetics, and the demarcation line is blurred. Naming hinges on puns and homonyms, the erratic side of logos that cannot be dissociated from its clear-cut side of straight meaning. And if I make a long shot – so does the Freudian unconscious, always using puns and homonyms to pave the way to its coming out and convey its erratic truth. There is a real of language that emerges in the midst of this, quite beyond its capacity to convey sense.

Of course we the moderns swear by Saussure, firmly believing that names, as all signs, are arbitrary and that any foundation of names in similarity is complete nonsense, fomenting fantasies that have no linguistic or epistemological value. Yet, can there ever be a word, a sign, an utterance, that we could simply take as arbitrary, with no other value than that? Isn't it rather that we are all profoundly Cratylian at heart, that words contingently connect, secretly correspond and form echoes, that they constantly produce fantasies by their sounds, that any sign or word, as arbitrary as it may be, ceases to be just arbitrary the moment we use it? And even if we officially agree with Hermogenes that names are just conventions, established by usage, this is not a view that we can ever espouse in our inner beliefs, dreams and desires. Names evoke, and what they evoke is not quite what they name. If the fancy foundations of names seem fantastic, then it is equally fantastic to assume that we will ever be able to reduce names to their reference. Names have their own power, and what the Janšas' project displays is this strange power, suspended between reference, evocation, desire, social fabric, and by their power they have the capacity to stir the network of power as such.

Cratylus, as the story goes, was allegedly Plato's first teacher of philosophy, his master, before he found his second and ultimate teacher in Socrates. So in this dialogue we have, like a condensation, Plato's two masters confronting each other and entering into a philosophical dispute, with Socrates duly taking the upper hand. But this is not the last of Cratylus. It seems that Cratylus, in his own way, has followed Socrates' advice of silently getting to the essence of things independent of names, giving up on names altogether. We can read the following subsequent testimony in Aristotle:

"Because they saw that all this world of nature is in movement, and that about that which changes no true statement can be made, they said that of course, regarding that which everywhere in every respect is changing, nothing could truly be affirmed. This belief that blossomed into the most extreme of the views ... was held by Cratylus, who finally did not think it right to say anything but only moved his finger, and criticized Heraclitus for saying that it is impossible to step twice into the same river; for he thought one could not do it even once." (*Metaphysics*, Book 4, 1010a)[9]

So there we have the extreme edge of philosophy, the sheer impossibility to say anything, the reduction of philosophy to merely moving a finger in silence, the ultimate gesture beyond the traps of logos and names. Moving a finger for merely pointing at things that one cannot name? Or is it rather the universally understandable gesture of raising the middle finger? Perhaps, in the Janšas' project, one should combine the two strategies: that of replicating the name and thus aiming

---

9   I am using *The Basic Works of Aristotle*, ed. Richard McKeon, New York: Random House, 2001.

at virtually replicating the bearer, and Cratylus' silent gesture of the middle finger.

Plato doesn't make any difference between proper names and common names. For him it's all the same whether we discuss the provenance and the aptitude of proper names such as Athena, Apollo, Hector, Astyanax, Janša, or common names such as truth, man, body, soul, knowledge, etc. The problem of the proper foundation of a name is the same. But this is not how this problem has generally been treated in linguistics and the philosophy of language, ancient or modern. It is obvious that common names can have vocabulary definitions which explain the meaning of a word by the properties of the entity it refers to, so that every word can be accounted for in terms of the traits that define its essential features. Every common name can be explained by a bunch of other common names, spelling out the characteristics that determine its meaning.[10] It is not quite so with proper names, or at least they present a special case. The first one can say is that they are not defined by common properties alone, one

---

10   A haphazard example from the net: "truth: the real facts about something; the things that are true; the quality or state of being true; a statement or idea that is true or accepted as true." This already displays the problem of all definitions being ultimately circular.

has to add some unique properties which single out its referent in its singularity. Say, the date and place of birth, profession and achievements. Yet these singular features that pertain exclusively to the bearer of the name and to no other person or entity don't quite behave in the same way as do the common features defining common names. If the name 'dog' refers to a set of properties that define that animal's particular nature, distinguishing it from other animals, thus delimiting the particular essence of the dog, say its 'dogeity', what makes a dog a dog, then the name Fido, referring to this singular dog bearing that name, doesn't define its 'fidoity' – there is no essence to this name, apart from the contingent act of nomination performed by its owner. Nor does the dog Fido share any features with the host of other animals that may carry the same name. The name is not a property like any other,[11] it is arbitrarily given, but the question is then: does the name function simply as shorthand for a set of properties that exhaustively describe the creature bearing that name?

---

11   There is an old joke about socialism as the synthesis of the highest achievements of the whole of human history to date: from prehistoric societies it took primitivism; from the Ancient world it took slavery; from medieval society brutal domination; from capitalism exploitation; and from socialism it took the name. The funny sting of this joke (used on some occasions by Slavoj Žižek) is that it takes the name to be a property like any other.

I don't want to enter at all into the long and fascinating discussion which opposed the descriptivist theory of proper names (whose most prominent proponent was Bertrand Russell), claiming that proper names can be reduced to a cluster of descriptions, and on the other hand the harsh critics of such a theory (most prominently Saul Kripke, whose *Naming and Necessity* (1980) is the most notorious book on the subject), claiming that a proper name is ultimately always a 'rigid designator', irreducible to a set of descriptions and properties, based solely on the contingent act of naming rigidly designating its object. Let me take a by-pass. If we take a name like 'Slovene', then it refers to a set of descriptions – geographical, historical, linguistic, demographic, etc. – but also to a set of some supposed real or imaginary properties – the Slovenes being diligent, disciplined, hard-working, conscientious, freedom-loving, friendly, god-fearing, proud, etc. (or else pompous, arrogant, envious, conceited, self-hating, self-righteous, take your pick). In this way, the name 'Slovene' would be shorthand for these descriptions, the function of the name would be nothing else but wrapping them up in a bundle and bringing them together under the same heading. The name is empty in itself, it is just a sack of elements, it refers to nothing by itself outside of these traits. But is this ever the case? It is rather that the empty signifier designates some mysterious property x which is irreducible to any of the traits, it is rather that one is prey to an inversion, a structural illusion, that all the properties appear to be but emanations of that enigmatic property x which is designated merely by the name. There is the specter of 'Sloveneness' which cannot be quite spelled out by the properties and which is pinned down by the name alone, not any of the positive traits.[12] 'Sloveneness' is ineffable, undefinable, unfathomable, inscrutable, immeasurable, it produces the phantom of indescribable depth just by being a pure effect of the empty gesture of naming. The name, beyond all properties, beyond the descriptivist account of proper names, refers to an x as its proper referent, a singular unnamable substance (as opposed to common names which inhabit different degrees of universality and particularity, and are in principle not singular). It creates an x, which is an ineffable being

---

12   I am borrowing this example freely from the only book by Slavoj Žižek devoted largely to Slovenes, *Jezik, ideologija, Slovenci*, Ljubljana: Delavska enotnost, 1987.

without properties, a nothing which neverthe-less appears as something, it never goes up in smoke by reduction to descriptions, it persists in its nothingness and provides the pure stuff of fantasies.[13]

It is thus with every name. No name without a specter. Naming is evoking a phantom, con-juring a ghost. One always names more than a cluster of descriptions, the singular ineffable x is there accompanying the use of names. The name always names the unnamable, or rather by naming it always produces the unnamable, something that cannot be captured by a mere name as shorthand for descriptive traits. The real of the name is what escapes naming, yet stands at its core.[14]

---

13   All this can be most economically clarified by the Lacanian algebra of S1/S2. S2 stands for the chain of properties, all of which make sense, while S1 stands for 'the signifier without a signified', a senseless signifier sustained merely by the act of nomination and its contingency. The proper referent of S1 would then be precisely the object 'a' and its unfathomable being.

14   A great literary testimony to this is Marcel Proust, with his ample rumi-nations about the images evoked by the names of various places, the phan-tasmatic cities, their particular flavors and aura, the dreamed up countries, conjured by the mere name. And of course, once he set foot in some of those places, it all evaporated, there was a structurally necessary bitter disappoint-ment, the place looked so different from what its name so vividly evoked. The phantom induced by the name is very central to Proust's enterprise – consider just the title of the third part of the first volume, *Le nom de pays: le nom (The Name of the Country: The Name)*, corresponding to the part of the second volume entitled *Le nom de pays: le pays (The Name of the Country: The Country)*.

If we try to pin down the name Janez Janša to a set of positive descriptions, one stumbles on a problem at the outset. One could try "the man born on 17 September 1958 in Ljubljana, twice Slovene prime minister, sentenced to prison on corruption charges, the hero of Slovene independence" etc., but the trouble is that this person doesn't bear the name Janez Janša, but Ivan Janša. Everything may be correct, except for the name, the prerequisite of definite description. It all seems that Janša is 'always already' redoubled, redoubled from the outset, in himself, known by a name which is not the name of his documents or birth certificate, making a career under an assumed name, thus presenting a good conundrum for the analytical philosophers of language (I am sure Kripke would have loved this and would eagerly include this case in one of his books). The singularity of naming coupled with the singularity of the date and place of birth is already inscribed into a wider social web of recognition, of 'also known as', 'aka', of an assumed and socially recognized identity, apart from the rigid designator attested by documents. Paradoxically, the three Janšas didn't replicate his name at all, they replicated its double, and since they really possess documents to prove that they are

Janez Janša, they 'really' are the legitimate bearers of this name, while the original is an impostor.[15] But what is a 'real' name? Can a name, freely given to people by choice, be 'real' in the sense that other entities are, entities named by the Other, the Platonic name-giver, the supposed divine namer, where we have no choice and no say? Do the official attestation and the documents vouchsafe for the reality of a name?

But maybe the real of a name, apart from its irreducible sound value, rather resides in the phantom that is evoked by it, the singular nameless substance it points to. This enigmatic feature is perhaps at the bottom of the unease produced by the name-change of the three Janšas, for if the ineffable x is singular, pertaining to that name only in its singularity, then the replication of the name causes some havoc by intervening in this singular substance. It is not that the singular person Janez Janša (aka Ivan Janša) would be affected by this replication – why would a politician of some standing care about some crazy

---

15   Even more: the three Janšas were issued birth certificates from which it follows that they have been born as Janez Janša, by the effect of the name change they have always already been Janez Janša. Name is endowed with a retroactive causality, it is not only a harbinger of a new future career, but also transforms the past.

artists changing their names? It is rather that the mysterious singular substance is affected the moment there are more pretenders to it. And if this property x of Janez Janša can be referred to as Janšeity (inadequately, for it pertains to its essence that it cannot be named), then it appears that the three new pretenders raise a claim precisely to Janšeity and they threaten to dispossess the one and true agent with a proper claim to it. They threaten to deprive him not of his unique name (for no name is unique), but by willfully embracing this name and replicating it they threaten to divest him of his substance, the x, that what is more in him than his name and its descriptive traits, the unnamable treasure and the aura.

Let us now approach names from a very different angle, that of a name-giver and the relation of names to posterity. We can all at some point step into the shoes of the Platonic name-giver and choose names of our children, and the names that we choose will stick to their fates, for better or worse, it depends on our whim how they will 'really' be called, we can arbitrarily mark them, and they will have to make do with that fateful mark, live up to it, revolt against it, love it or hate it, but there can be no indifference, names inspire passions that one cannot escape. One striking example will suffice.

Freud had six children, three sons and three daughters. To list them by the order of birth: Mathilde (1887), Jean-Martin (1889), Oliver (1891), Ernst (1892), Sophie (1893), Anna (1895). Freud insisted to choose the names of the children himself. This is how he commented on this in *The Interpretation of Dreams*:

> "I had insisted on their names [of my children] being chosen, not according to the fashion of the moment, but in memory of people I have been fond of. Their names made the children into *revenants*. [*Ihre Namen machen die Kinder zu Revenants.*] And after all, I reflected, was not having children our own path to immortality?" (PFL 2, p. 487; SA II, pp. 468–9)[16]

This is a most curious remark. To follow its logic, children would actually be like ghosts, the revenants, for their names are chosen on the model

16 *The Pelican Freud Library* (PFL), 15 vols., London: Penguin, 1973–86; *Studienausgabe* (SA), 10 vols., Frankfurt/M: Fischer, 1969–75.

of the people we care for so that they would live their afterlife for them, they are by their names doomed to be the impersonations of the dead.[17] Their life already starts as an afterlife, they are ghosts with a mission. Freud, by choosing the names himself, fully exerted his paternal authority on this point as an authority of naming. The name pertains to the father.

So who were the models? First for the sons: Jean-Martin was named after Jean-Martin Charcot, Freud's great teacher and master in matters of psychiatry, with whom he spent a most formative year at the Salpêtrière Hospital in Paris in 1885–6; Oliver was named after Oliver Cromwell, for whom Freud always harbored a great admiration;[18] and Ernst after Ernst Brücke,

---

17   At the point of their naming, four out of six models were actually alive. Nevertheless, the point is that children are destined to survive the models after which they have been named, and carry on the torch for them, they are named as already the revenants (literally those who come back), even though of the living.

18   Freud was anything but naïve, so he commented on this choice in the following manner: "... my second son, to whom I had given the first name of a great historical figure [Oliver Cromwell] who had powerfully attracted me in my boyhood, especially since my visit to England. During the year before the child's birth, I had made up my mind to use this name if it were a son and I greeted the newborn baby with a feeling of high satisfaction. (It is easy to see how the suppressed megalomania of fathers is transferred in their thoughts on to their children, and it seems quite probable that this is one of the ways in which the suppression of that feeling, which becomes necessary in actual life, is carried out.)" (Quoted from http://www.freud.org.uk/education/dream/63806/garibaldi-dream/)

Freud's first great teacher and master in matters of natural science who died three months before the son's birth – Freud spent 'the happiest years of his life' in Brücke's physiological laboratory in 1876–81.[19] As for the daughters, Mathilde was named after Mathilde Breuer (born Altmann), the wife of Josef Breuer, Freud's closest friend and collaborator at the time; Sophie after Sophie Schwab-Paneth, a close friend of the family; and Anna after Anna Hammerschlag-Lichtheim, another close family friend and famously Freud's patient – she was the notorious Irma of the dream of Irma's injection, Freud's most famous specimen dream. What the three women had in common was that they were the godmothers to the three daughters.

One cannot but be a bit perplexed: the sons after great scientists and political heroes, the daughters after the friends of the family who eagerly assumed the roles of godmothers. Freud, the great revolutionary, the great discoverer and innovator, was at the same time deeply footed in the 19th century with his very private web of fantasies

---

19   Freud's grandson, the great painter Lucian Freud, was Ernst's son, and in line with the tradition of the family he was duly named after his mother (Lucie Brasch).

which conditioned naming, this short-circuit between the most private and the public. Any parent who ever named his or her child knows about the anxiety that comes with naming, the intricate mixture of private fixations and fantasies, personal fancies and fixed ideas, the imaginary aura that surrounds various names, and on the other hand, of the public emblem that the child will have to carry throughout his/her life.

But the intriguing and interesting thing in Freud's remark is the connection that he makes between names and immortality. Having children is our way to immortality, the continuation of our lives through our offspring. But this is not enough, what is at stake is not merely a biological survival of an individual by proxy, there is the question of symbolic transmission by names. The genus will go on and may extend the present individual into possible immortality through his progeny, our genes may be infinitely replicated – an individual may be seen as a gene's way to create another gene, its double – genes are indeed selfish, to follow Richard Dawkins,[20] they only care about their own reproduction, we

---

20   Richard Dawkins, *The Selfish Gene*, Oxford University Press, 1976.

are just a means to their ends. Our biological singularity, inscribed in the unique signature of our DNA, may thus be indefinitely continued and prolonged. But the name is like our cultural DNA, the unique mark of our singular inscription into the social, and naming children after our heroes and our beloved ones is propelled by the hope that our cultural DNA may run at least a small part of the way alongside with our biological DNA into the unforeseeable future. The individual name may be seen as a signifier's way to provide its replica, its cultural progeny, the individual is the name's way to make another name. Generically, this holds for family names which generally bear the imprint of the name of the father, the supposed head of the family and the supposed name-giver, but this also holds for the private trade, so to speak, in individual given names, freely chosen, but inspired by the same mission, although in far less predictable ways, prompted by personal enthusiasms, fantasies, preferences and inclinations.

If the name raises claims to immortality, then Janez Janša may perhaps not be so enthusiastic about being immortalized by these particular replications of his name. Although, who knows, it may prove that they ultimately present a better chance at his immortality than his political career. In the long run, art may last longer than politics.

There is another way that the name is connected to immortality. Brecht speaks somewhere about Hegel, his great Teacher in the matters of the Great Method, i.e. dialectics. He ascribes to him "the abilities of one of the greatest humorists among philosophers", especially since he was particularly interested in how things constantly change into their opposites and can never remain the same. "He contested that one equals one, not only because everything that exists inexorably and persistently passes into something else, namely its opposite, but because nothing at all is identical to itself. As any humorist, he was especially interested in what becomes of things. As the Berlin saying goes: 'My, how you have changed, Emil!'"[21] At this point the kind publisher provides a footnote, explaining that this is taken from a Berlin joke in which a widow visits the grave of her late husband and addresses his gravestone with these words. The example

21   *Flüchtlingsgespräche, Gesammelte Werke*, vol. 14, Frankfurt/M.: Suhrkamp, 1982, p. 1460.

of dialectics par excellence: everything changes, for example, Emil has turned into a gravestone bearing his name. (It was not me who came up with the name Emil here, it was Brecht, who wrote it referring to Berlin folklore.)

When they changed their names, the three Janez Janšas, and especially the one who dialectically 'is and is not' Emil ('namely' Emil Hrvatin), kept pointing out, among other things, that the change of one's name carries the connotation of a symbolic death. If you change your name, it is as if you've died, as if you've experienced your own death in the (symbolic) relation to others.[22] Brecht's joke presents the flip-side of the matter: the bearer changes, even more, passes away and disappears in the most literal way, but what remains is precisely his name. He has 'really' died, but the name symbolically survived. No matter how drastically the state of the bearer changes in this alteration, the name remains the same and persists. The name is that which will outlive us,

---

22   Most curiously, the online *Glossary of Slovene Art* 1945–2005 (www.pojmovnik.si) features brief entries on the three artists prior to their name change, and it undauntedly states 2007 as the year of their death. Emil Hrvatin (1964–2007), Davide Grassi (1970–2007) and Žiga Kariž (1973–2007). The fact that the latter eventually changed his name again to its previous form didn't resurrect him from the dead in the impartial eyes of the *Glossary* big Other.

it is more enduring than we are, it presents our chance at immortality. It will outlive us, first in the general sense, as inscribed in the symbolic order and thus serve as a reference point for what we might be remembered for, but then in a more banal and directly material sense, as written on a gravestone, i.e. literally carved in stone. A name is something that imprints our identity into stone and makes it indelible. Names are endowed with a secret plot – the word that in English also means a family tomb (Hitchcock's last film was entitled Family Plot and it played precisely on this double meaning of the word). They have a secret mission, a destination, the name being that part of us that will one day find itself on our gravestone. The name's secret intent is, among other things, to be carved into the gravestone, into the endurable substance, virtually unchangeable, at least as far as can be foreseen. It is that part of our identity that is more lasting than we are, written on the supposedly most lasting substance of stone. Names are 'eternal', we are not, names last, we pass away. The free choice of the name change has its flip-side, the non-choice regarding the gravestone where the name would eventually be carved, the immortal part of our mortal selves, and the context of the symbolic death accompanying the name-change has its flip side in symbolic survival. The name symbolically continues to live its life beyond our lives, it presents the real of our lives beyond our bodily life. On the one hand, there is the part whereby the bearer remains the same, unchanged, and can freely change his names at his whim, without this affecting his or her substance (at least seemingly), but on the other hand, there is the part where the name vindicates itself from beyond the grave, proving to outlast its bearer, who may change his substance but not his name. The name proves to be more 'substantial' and endurable than the passing bearer. We are but a brief episode in the long life of our names.

There is a 200-year-old French saying: "There is no room for two Napoleons." It has several variations, e.g. "at the top, there is not enough space for two Napoleons" or "France is not big enough for two Napoleons." If someone claims to be Napoleon, then this is a clear case of a lunatic that has to be put in an asylum – hence also the archetypal idea of a lunatic claiming to be Napoleon.[23] And since this particular name

---

23   According to Lacan's famous adage, the madman is not the poor wretch who believes himself to be a king, but the true madman in the king who >>>

change does not involve just any name but the name of the prime minister, then in light of this adage it entails a question: is Slovenia big enough not for two, but for four Napoleons?[24] Should the three surplus Napoleons, the Napoleon extras, who zealously claim that they, too, are Napoleons and prove this with documents, be put in an asylum? Or is this an 'art project', thus a modern alternative to the asylum, since in art, supposedly, everything is allowed and the most preposterous ideas can be even highly socially valued? Where do they belong – in an asylum or in a gallery? Or should they be put in prison, like their model, the Slovene ex-prime minister who eventually landed in prison in June 2014, convicted of corruption? What is the status of 'art' in this immediate meddling into the structure of power and its names?

The 'art project', if this is one, poses a most 'real' question that relates nomination and domination. The question is not what qualifies some-

believes himself to be a king. It may be said that a considerable part of Slovene political problems stems from having such a case in our midst.

24   On a more trivial level, the three Janšas experienced quite a few practical difficulties when they couldn't travel together on a plane because the computer cancelled their surplus tickets, assuming that three passengers with the same name must be an error. So there is no room for two Napoleons even on a plane.

one to bear, e.g. the name Žiga Kariž, but what qualifies someone bearing, e.g. the name Janez Janša to occupy the position of power. What is the intricate connection between a name and power? Is power without a name possible? Is a name not inscribed in power relations possible? Is there such a thing as a neutral and innocent name? A name is always the bearer of a symbolic mandate and as soon as there appear false pretenders, with the documents and all, the question is raised about the validity and the justification of the symbolic mandate enabling power. Names, to be sure, refer to genealogies, but through that they always involve a certain distribution of power. To arrogate a name is to arrogate power.

Here is a true story, an episode from Russian history. The story of Boris Godunov, the Russian regent and then the Russian tsar (in the period 1598–1605), was immortalized first by Pushkin's drama (1831) and then most notably by Mussorgsky's opera (1869/72), one of the most impressive operas in history. It prominently features the episode of the false Dmitry, the pretender to the throne. The story goes that Boris Godunov had a tsarevich Dmitry murdered in 1591 (this was the youngest son of

Ivan the Terrible) in his lust for power (although modern historians have doubts about this), and once Godunov became the tsar there appeared a pretender (around 1600) who claimed to be the tsarevich who escaped the assassination.[25] The false Dmitry, seen as a threat and a nuisance by Godunov, fled to Poland where he gathered considerable support and converted to Catholicism to secure the help of Vatican. He entered Russia with his small army in 1604, where a lot of people joined him in his campaign against the unpopular tsar. His army grew, he was initially victorious until his luck changed and he suffered some bad defeats. But when Godunov died in 1605, the tides changed again, so eventually the supposed Dmitry triumphantly entered Moscow surrounded by a mass of followers and was duly crowned as the new tsar Dmitry. The name worked, the name was enough for the claim to power and for the successful accession, although the guy was certainly an impostor, most probably a monk called Grigory Otrepyev. Once on the throne, he married his beloved Polish lady Marina Mniszech, who'd helped him all along.

---

25   In Russian, as in Slovene, the pretender is called *samozvanec*, literally someone who calls himself by a name, someone who gives himself a name, a self-namer. He is not called by that name by the others, but by his own whim.

But the tides soon changed again, his Catholicism was a bit too much for Russia, he was assassinated in 1606 along with his supporters and a new tsar was appointed, Vassily IV. But this was not all: soon a second pretender turned up, the false Dmitry II, again gathering considerable support of Poles and Cossacks, putting up a sizeable army and an armed camp at Tushino. He, too, had some military success, he tried to seize Moscow but didn't quite manage – although the deposed tsarina Marina, the widow of the first Dmitry, recognized him as the genuine reincarnation of her first husband, claiming that this was the same man. He was assassinated in his own turn in 1610. But this was not all: in 1611, yet another false pretender appeared, the false Dmitry III, again securing some support, the Cossacks acknowledged him as the tsar, but he soon followed the gory fate of his two predecessors in 1612. The hapless widow yet again miraculously recognized the third pretender as the true one, her one and only husband. Can one be married to a name? Here is a lady who married the name Dmitry, she was faithfully married to this one name throughout her life, it just so happened that it had three different bearers, all of them impostors. The story is fascinating, it appealed not only to the Russians (above all Pushkin and Mussorgsky, but quite a few others), but also to, say, Schiller (with his unfinished drama Demetrius) and Rilke (where the story features in his Malte Laurids Brigge).

And as if all this was not enough, the story was reenacted once more in the Russian 20th century, with the appearance in 1920 of 'princess' Anastasia, the supposed youngest daughter of the assassinated last tsar Nicolas, the Grand Duchess who claimed to have escaped assassination and then divided the Russian exile community into a bunch of firm believers and the majority of skeptical opponents. The story was immortalized by Hollywood (Ingrid Bergman got an Oscar for this role in 1956). The lady tried hard to prove her case throughout her life, which entailed one of the longest lawsuits in history, but she was eventually turned down in 1970 on the basis of insufficient evidence. As it turned out, with the DNA analysis in 1994, she was an impostor, her name was actually Anna Anderson. But of course she was not the only one, some ten women claimed to be the Grand Duchess Anastasia.[26]

---

26   The theme of impostors looms large in Russian culture. Just remember Khlestakov in Gogol's amazing *The Government Inspector (Revizor)* or >>>

The false pretenders assumed the royal name in their claim to power (or to social prestige), and it all ended in bloodshed (or in shame). What's in a name? How come the mere name can lead to so much blood and havoc? The least one can say is that names are not to be taken lightly – there is always the moment of the claim to power in every name, in the assumption of the social role that goes along with it, in the transmission of symbolic legacy, in the social impact, in the inscription into a genealogy, and the royal false pretenders only display this in a particularly salient manner. But their stories also entail the flip-side, the moment of bemusement whereby one has the feeling that one is actually always a false pretender, and a false pretender to a royal name that should be vindicated only brings forth some part of our common fate. For there is no way one could inhabit a name legitimately, naturally, with ease, by being fully justified to bear the name one bears. There is no sufficient ground to bear a name, it can never be substantiated, no name is ever covered by the Leibnizian principle of sufficient reason. Proper

---

Chichikov in his *Dead Souls*, or the notorious figure of Ostap Bender in Ilf and Petrov, the proverbial impostor who started to function as an epitome of something deeply planted in 'the Russian soul'.

names, as opposed to common names, can always be other than they are, one is free to choose and to change them, or such is the necessary illusion (while common names are fixed by the dictionary and consensus). The feeling of being an impostor, a false pretender to the name, is not some personal sentiment or idiosyncrasy, it is a structural feeling that accompanies names as their shadow and effect.

The three Janšas, by their name-change, may look something like a reenactment of the three false Dmitrys. They brought to the fore both aspects, the name as a claim to power, the tacit distribution of power that goes along with names, and on the other hand, the false pretense, the impersonation that accompanies the functioning of names. One is always the impersonator of one's own name. Their name-change raised the question not only of them being false pretenders to the name of Janez Janša, but also of Janez Janša being a false pretender to his own name and to its stakes in power. They never disclosed their motives (claiming personal reasons and, at the most, artistic ambitions), never raised a claim to power (as opposed to the Dmitrys), but always maintained (in accordance with the Dmitrys) that they were 'real' Janez Janšas, which they could prove with their documents, and that is more than their model can do. But by desisting from reasons and justifications, both the implied web of power and the 'structural' impersonation came all the more to the fore.

In Slovene history, the memory of the time when people massively changed their names and assumed new ones is still very alive. These were the so-called 'partisan names' during the time of the anti-fascist struggle, the assumed names that were based on the tradition of using fictitious names in the circumstances of conspiratorial and illegal activities, covering up 'real' identities in order to protect their bearers. But, on the other hand, this justification does not explain everything, for behind the pragmatic justification there lurks a different desire and will, a desire and a will to found a new symbolic order, a new order of designations and symbolic mandates where the 'real' and the symbolic impact no longer lie in the real name, but in a newly chosen and assumed partisan name, which is destined to be the bearer of the real identity, regardless of the official documents. One can be reminded that the revolutionary will of the French Revolution expressed itself in, among other things, a new calendar and the new designations of months, among which the best known is perhaps Brumaire (and Thermidor and Germinal), since the above-mentioned Napoleon assumed power on 18 Brumaire, while Marx immortalized this date in the eponymous essay referring to the other Napoleon, Napoleon's nephew, who, in the historical farcical repetition, relied precisely on the mandate of his name – another false pretender but bearing the 'real' name. For a more direct precedent, one can evoke Vladimir Ilyich Ulyanov changing his name to Lenin, Lev Davidovich Bronstein to Trotsky and Iossif Vissarionovich Dzhugashvili to Stalin. And Josip Broz to Tito. The will for a symbolic cut, a radical shift in the symbolic fabric of society, manifests itself as the will to renaming.

The name change of the three Janez Janšas is, in a certain way, inscribed into the tradition of the partisan struggle, assuming partisan names, since these new names – three identical ones, contrary to tradition – apart from involving a very practical official change of all the documents, also had the effect of the foundation of a parallel symbolic space, of a virtual new designation and thus the perspective of a different symbolic relation that blurs the delimitation of art, civil status and political mandate. The impact was conditioned precisely in the disregard of the delimitation of these areas and in their coincidence in the same gesture.

The choice of partisan names was not arbitrary; they always carry a symbolic mandate, although they are seemingly chosen only according to the criterion of having no connection with the real name. It is quite astounding that Edvard Kardelj chose Krištof for his partisan name, which after all carries the whole connotation of St. Christopher, whose symbolic mission was to carry Christ – hence his name (carrier of Christ) and his iconic representation in innumerable variants with the child Christ on his shoulders. And this was also what this highest Communist Party luminary dutifully took upon himself, being the second-in-command at Tito's side and his firmest support through decades. The foundation of assuming a new name has biblical dimensions; it extends to the sources of naming, the authority of giving names, back to Adam. The assumed name is now the real name, an inscription into an alternative symbolic network, in opposition to the arbitrariness of civil identity based on spurious authority. The virtual inscription redoubles the ordinary inscription and undermines its symbolic sway.

From this point of view, the context of a name change is not only the context of a symbolic death, but at the same time the context of a new birth. Its biblical dimension is not accidental since renaming was often connected precisely with conversion, with adopting a new religion, with the sudden enlightenment and the new baptism. To take just one notorious example: Cassius Clay, the most famous boxer in history, changed his name to Mohamed Ali and thus marked his conversion to Islam. 'Born again', as the phrase goes, and being born again into the new faith entails a new baptism and the possibility of choosing a new name. Thus also the partisan names marked a conversion to a new belief and entailed a new birth, a baptism, a metamorphosis.[27]

---

27   In a strange and somewhat vertiginous counterpart, Adolf Hitler's story also involves a name change. His father was born as Alois Schickelgruber (1837–1903), and having been born out of wedlock he assumed his mother's name. In 1876, thirteen years before Adolf's birth, he made an official request to change his surname to Hiedler, which was the name of his step-father (who subsequently married his mother and might actually have been his biological father, although the evidence is flimsy). When the name change was entered into the official registry in 1877 it was changed to Hitler, for reasons unknown. The biggest stroke of luck in Hitler's entire career thus happened a dozen years before he was born, through the choice made not by him but by his father, concerning precisely 'the Name of the Father' – can one imagine masses chanting 'Heil Schickelgruber'? What's in a name? There is a name which >>>

The renaming of the three Janez Janšas caused unease precisely because the three bearers of the new name at no moment wanted to explain their decision and provide the reason for their name change. (But, ultimately, what would be a sufficient reason for any naming?) They did not substantiate or justify the name change with conversion, the adoption of a new belief, the beginning of new life or by claiming that, until then, their lives had been misguided. And the name they had chosen didn't seem to embody their belief, their political allegiance, or to provide a model of what they wanted to be. Anything but – yet even if we can assume that it perhaps embodies precisely all that they themselves would by no means want to be, they kept completely quiet about it, no criticism was ever explicitly voiced. Faced with the media probing, the only reasons they kept repeating were 'personal reasons', an intimate personal decision, etc., that is, something that functions as a cloak behind which it is impolite to probe, but at the same time as a cliché excuse, since 'per-

most often condenses and metaphorises a political movement, but it cannot be any odd name, it has to possess some evocative power and the striking sound value. No matter how persuasive the ideas and how viable the political program, there has to be a persuasive and viable name as their figurehead. The contingent sound value of a name is never contingent, it possesses the power to stir imagination and fantasies, a name is never arbitrary. Witness the caricature name Schickelgruber, as if cut out for a character in a farce.

sonal reasons' are precisely another name for not wanting to reveal the true reason. The lack of justification for the name change, the fact that it was not accompanied by a conversion to some new faith, the cloning of three identical names that precisely excludes individuality and uniqueness and, lastly, the choice of the name that does not borrow from any celebrated and mythical past, but points to the not-so-glorious present – all this makes it impossible to make sense of this gesture and its message in any immediate or obvious way. The gesture obviously has a strong message, but it is not quite clear what this message is supposed to be. And lastly, if – as with partisan names – these name changes evoke the will for a new symbolic mandate and a different foundation, the gesture of a symbolic cut, then this alleged new symbolic order here presents itself precisely as the cloning of the most notorious name around, that of the bearer of the ruling order at the time, and it looks as if mere cloning undermines the model. The new is only the gap in the contingency of the old, the sameness of names points to an arbitrary coincidence of the bearer and the name, as if a new version of the Hegelian infinite judgment was at work here, which asserts a direct identity of entities that have no common measure: Janez

Janša = Janez Janša = Janez Janša = Janez Janša. Or, in another vein, not unlike 'a rose is a rose is a rose ... is a rose.'

One cannot finish without evoking the best-known scene in the entirety of theatre history, the canonical *locus princeps* of the theatrical tradition, the theatre scene *par excellence*. Juliet stands on the balcony and speaks into the night, and on this most famous spot, she says: "What's in a name?"[28] Wouldn't the rose by any other name smell as sweet? "O Romeo, Romeo! Wherefore art thou Romeo? / Deny thy father and refuse thy name." This is not the question of changing the name, but the question of an exit from the regime of names altogether, the departure from the symbolic places assigned to us by names. But such a way out is not possible, hence the tragedy of the Verona lovers.

The scene pits one against the other: on the one hand, the absolute demand of love, and on the other hand, something one could call the politics of the name. Every name entails a politics. By

---

28   "What's in a name? That which we call a rose / By any other name would smell as sweet; / So Romeo would, were he not Romeo call'd, / Retain that dear perfection which he owes / Without that title. Romeo, doff thy name; / And for that name, which is no part of thee, / Take all myself." (II, 2, 43–49)

one's name one always belongs to a certain social group, a class, a nation, a family, the names pin us down to an origin, a genealogy, a tradition, names classify us and allot us a social place, they distribute social power. By the name, one is always a Montague or a Capulet ("and I'll no longer be a Capulet," says Juliet). By our names, we are always inscribed in social antagonisms, they always place us either on the Montague or on the Capulet side.

A name is never individual, it is always generic. By the family name, we are always placed under the banner of the father's name, the Name of the Father, so with the family name we always carry around psychoanalysis and all its luggage. But also the given name is never personal, it is inscribed into a code – in our culture it is precisely the 'Christian name', traditionally given according to the date of birth and its patron saint, based on a ramified classification of saintly distribution. Or else excluded from it – Ivan Cankar's remarkable short story *Polikarp*, just a hundred years old, tells the story of a man who was given this curious name, Polikarp, at his birth, in order to stigmatize him as a child born out of wedlock, a bastard. He was doomed to carry that name as his mark of Cain, the name defined his fate from his birth to the bitter end. Although nowadays the codes of naming are more relaxed, elusive and loose, seemingly liberal, they still very much exist and continue to secretly delineate us, although in subtle ways that are hard to decipher.

Where does the name reside? "It is nor hand, nor foot, / Nor arm, nor face, nor any other part / Belonging to a man," says Juliet, and further: "'Tis but thy name that is my enemy." So everything would be all right, or so it seems, if only he could cut off his name, the source of all trouble, and this is what he indeed attempts to do at some point. "In what vile part of this anatomy / Doth my name lodge?" asks Romeo later in the play (III/3). "Tell me that I may sack / The hateful mansion." And he draws his sword, as the stage directions indicate, prepared to cut off that vile bodily part, to cut off his name with the sword, castrate himself of his name, the name of the Father,[29] but to no avail. To cut off the name

_____
29   What part of the body might he purport to cut off when he draws his sword? Does he tacitly assume that 'the phallic signifier' resides in his phallus? Is this not the spontaneous assumption that the audience inevitably makes? This is like an almost caricature Lacanian *Urszene*, bringing together the Name of the Father, the phallic signifier, castration, and the nature of love. The fate of the Veronese lovers may actually be sealed by this assumption >>>

61

in order to espouse the immediacy. "Deny thy father and refuse thy name" – in order to fully assume love? This is the fantasy of the Verona lovers – love beyond names and signifiers, the communion of immediate being.

In the balcony scene, love appears as that which should entail leaving behind all these social codes. The tragedy of the Veronese lovers stems from the stark opposition between name and being, that unique human being which is supposed to be beyond naming and which should enable establishing a bond apart from names, the true bond of love and passion based on singularity. And this is at the core of their tragedy: the name has nevertheless affected their being and took revenge, they couldn't overcome the way they were marked by their proper names, there is no way one can cut off names as expendable additions, for names as intruders are nevertheless what gives us access to being, and they affect being.

Does Emil Hrvatin by the name Janez Janša smell the same? Will the name Janez Janša ever smell the same?

---

that true love resides in the immediacy, by getting rid of the phallic signifier of the name as the intruder into the purity of heart.

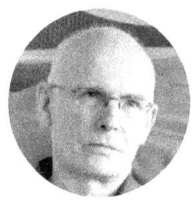

Mladen Dolar is Professor and Senior Research Fellow at the Department of Philosophy, University of Ljubljana. His principal areas of research are psychoanalysis, modern French philosophy, German idealism and art theory. He has lectured extensively at universities in the US and across Europe, he is the author of over a hundred papers in scholarly journals and volume collections. Apart from ten books in Slovene, his book publications include most notably A Voice and Nothing More (MIT 2006, translated into six languages) and Opera's Second Death (with Slavoj Žižek, Routledge 2001, also translated into several languages). He is the co-founder of what has become known as 'the Ljubljana School'.

www.ingramcontent.com/pod-product-compliance
Lightning Source LLC
Chambersburg PA
CBHW072243170526
45158CB00002BA/993